I0177515

PRACTICAL OBSERVATIONS

UPON THE

EDUCATION OF THE PEOPLE,

ADDRESSED TO

THE WORKING CLASSES

AND

THEIR EMPLOYERS.

BY

H. BROUGHAM, Esq. M.P. F.R.S.

TWENTIETH EDITION.

LONDON:

PRINTED BY RICHARD TAYLOR, SHOE-LANE;

AND SOLD BY LONGMAN, HURST, REES, ORME, BROWN, AND GREEN,

PATERNOSTER-ROW,

FOR THE BENEFIT OF THE LONDON MECHANICS INSTITUTION.

1825.

GEORGE BIRKBECK, M.D.

President of the London Mechanics Institution.

As I have chiefly in deference to your opinion, sanctioned by that of our fellow-labourers in the North, undertaken to make the following pages public at the present moment, I beg leave to inscribe them with your name.

You are aware that they contain a portion of a larger discourse, which more pressing but less agreeable pursuits have long prevented me from finishing, upon the important subject of Popular Education, in its three branches, Infant Schools, Elementary Schools (for reading and writing), and Adult Schools. It is only with the second of these branches that the Legislature can safely interfere. Any meddling on the part of Government with the first would be inexpedient; with the last, perilous to civil and religious liberty. In conformity with this opinion I have brought the question of Elementary Education repeatedly before Parliament, where the lukewarmness of many, and the honest and by me ever to be respected scruples of some, have hitherto much obstructed my design: the other two branches belong to the country at large. Having, in concert with those friends who hold the same doctrines, endeavoured to establish Infant Schools, it seems to follow from the same view of the subject, that I should lend any little help in my power towards fixing public attention upon the Education of Adults; by discussing the best means of aiding the people in using the knowledge gained at schools, for their moral and intellectual improvement.

A considerable portion of the Observations was inserted in the Edinburgh Review, together with a good deal of other matter, and with one or two statements in which I do not altogether concur.

PRACTICAL OBSERVATIONS,

&c.

I BEGIN by assuming that there is no class of the community so entirely occupied with labour as not to have an hour or two every other day at least, to bestow upon the pleasure and improvement to be derived from reading—or so poor as not to have the means of contributing something towards purchasing this gratification, the enjoyment of which, beside the present amusement, is the surest way both to raise our character and better our condition.—Let us consider how the attainment of this inestimable advantage may be most successfully promoted.

It is no doubt manifest, that the people themselves must be the great agents in accomplishing the work of their own instruction. Unless they deeply feel the usefulness of knowledge, and resolve to make some sacrifices for the acquisition of it, there can be no reasonable prospect of this grand object being attained. But it is equally clear, that to wait until the whole people with one accord take the determination to labour in this good work, would be endless. A portion of the community may be sensible of its advantages, and willing at any fair price to seek them, long before the same laudable feeling becomes universal; and their successful efforts to better their intellectual condition cannot fail to spread more widely the love of learning, and the disrelish for sensual and vulgar gratifications.

But although the people must be the source and the instruments of their own improvement, they may be essentially aided in their efforts to instruct themselves. Impediments which might be sufficient to retard or wholly to obstruct their progress, may be removed; and efforts which, unassisted, might prove fruitless, arising perhaps from a transient, or only a partial enthusiasm for the attainment of knowledge, may, through judicious encouragement, become effectual, and settle into a lasting and an universal habit. A little attention to the difficulties that principally beset the working classes in their search after information, will lead us to the knowledge both of the direction in which their more affluent neighbours can lend them most valuable assistance, and of the part which must be borne by themselves.

Their difficulties may all be classed under one or other of two heads—want of money, and want of time. To the first belongs the difficulty of obtaining those books and instructors which persons in easier circumstances can command; and to the second it is owing that the same books and instructors are not adapted to them, which suffice to teach persons who have leisure to go through the whole course of any given branch of science. In some lines of employment, there is a peculiar difficulty in finding time for acquiring knowledge; as in those which require severe labour, or, though less severe, yet in the open air; for here the tendency to sleep immediately after it ceases, and the greater portion of sleep required, oppose very serious obstacles to instruction: on the other hand those occupations are less unfavourable to reflection, and have a considerable tendency to enlarge the mind.

The first method, then, which suggests itself for promoting knowledge among the poor, is the encouragement of cheap publications; and in no country is this more wanted than in Great Britain, where, with all our expertness in manufactures, we have never succeeded in printing books at so little as double the price required by our neighbours on the continent. A gown, which any where else would cost half a guinea, may be made in this country for half a crown; but a volume, fully as well or better printed, and on paper which, if not as fine, is quite fine enough, and far more agreeable to the eyes, than could be bought in London for half a guinea, costs only six francs, or less than five shillings, at Paris. The high price of labour in a trade where so little can be done, or at least has been done by machinery, is one of the causes of this difference. But the direct tax upon paper is another; and the determination to print upon paper of a certain price is a third; and the aversion to crowd the page is a fourth. Now all of these, except the first, may be got over. The duty on paper is threepence a pound, which must increase the price of an octavo volume eightpence or ninepence; and this upon paper of every kind, and printing of every kind; so that if by whatever means the price of a book were reduced to the lowest, say to three or four shillings, about a fourth or a fifth must be added for the tax; and this book, brought as low as possible to accommodate the poor man, with the coarsest paper and most ordinary type, must pay exactly as much to government as the finest hot-pressed work of the same size. This tax ought, therefore, by all means, to be given up; but though, from its being the same upon all paper used in printing, no part of it can be saved by using coarse paper, much of it may be saved by crowding the letter-press, and having a very narrow margin. This experiment has been tried of late in London upon a considerable scale; but it may easily be carried a great deal further. Thus, Hume's History * has been begun; and one volume, containing about two

---

* It is to be regretted that any edition of this popular work should ever be published without notes, to warn the reader of the author's partiality when moved by the interest of civil and ecclesiastical controversy, and his careless and fanciful narrative when occupied with other events.

and a half of the former editions, has been published *. It is sold for six shillings and sixpence; but it contains a great number of cuts neatly executed; the paper is much better than is necessary; and the printing is perfectly well done. Were the cuts omitted, and the most ordinary paper and type used, the price might be reduced to 4s. or 4s. 6d.; and a book might thus be sold for 12s. or 14s., which now costs perhaps above two pounds. A repeal of the tax upon paper, which is truly a tax upon knowledge, and falls the heaviest upon those who most want instruction, would further reduce the price to nine or ten shillings.

The method of publishing in Numbers is admirably suited to the circumstances of the classes whose income is derived from wages. Twopence is easily saved in a week by almost any labourer; and by a mechanic sixpence in a week may without difficulty be laid by. Those who have not attended to such matters, would be astonished to find how substantial a meal of information may be had by twopenny-worths. Seven numbers, for fourteen pence, comprise Franklin's Life and Essays; four for eightpence, Bacon's Essays; and 36 for six shillings, the whole of the Arabian Nights. Cook's Voyages, in threepenny numbers, with many good engravings, may be had complete for seven shillings; and Plutarch's Lives, for ten shillings, will soon be finished †. The Mirror, a weekly publication, containing much matter of harmless and even improving amusement, selected with very considerable taste, has besides, in almost every number, information of a most instructive kind. Its great circulation must prove highly beneficial to the bulk of the people. I understand, that of some parts upwards of 80,000 were printed, and there can be no doubt that the entertainment which is derived from reading the lighter essays, may be made the means of conveying knowledge of a more solid and useful description—a consideration which I trust the conductor will always bear in mind. The Mechanics Magazine ‡, most ably edited by Mr. Robertson, has from its establishment, had an extensive circulation; and it communicates for threepence a week, far more valuable information, both scientific and practical, than was ever before placed within the reach of those who could afford to pay six times as much for it. A similar work is published at Glasgow upon the same plan. Upon a similar plan and at the same price a valuable work, called the " *Register of Arts and Sciences,*" has been published weekly for about eight months. The Chemist, also for threepence, is learnedly and judiciously conducted by Mr. Hodgkin, and contains an admirable collection of the most useful chemical papers and intelligence. A Mechanics Register has lately

---

* Dolby's cheap Histories.   † Limbird's Classics.

‡ Knight and Lacy; who have done great service by publishing other works of singular cheapness and merit. The Dictionary of Architecture is one of the most extraordinary in this respect.

been begun, and with immediate success. —It is a weekly paper, for the same price; and although, being principally intended for the use of the workmen, it bestows peculiar attention on whatever concerns that order, yet the occurrences which it communicates, and the discussions which it contains, are also those most interesting to philosophers themselves. The day, indeed, seems now to break, when we may hope to see no marked line of separation between the two classes. I trust another distinction will also soon be known no more. The circulation of cheap works of a merely amusing kind, as well as of those connected with the arts, is at present very great in England; those of an aspect somewhat more forbidding, though at once moral, interesting, and most useful, is very limited; while in Scotland there is a considerable demand for them. Habits of reading longer formed in that country, have taught the inhabitants, that nothing in reality can be more attractive than the profound wisdom of every day's application, sustained by unbounded learning, and embellished with the most brilliant fancy, which so richly furnishes every page of the Essays of Bacon.

It is undoubtedly from the circumstance just mentioned, that in looking over the list of those cheap publications, which are unconnected with the arts, we certainly do not find many that are of a very instructive cast; and here it is that something may be done by way of encouragement. That the demand for books, cheap as well as dear, must tend to produce them, no one denies; but then it is equally certain, that the publication of cheap books increases the number of readers among the poor; and one can hardly conceive a greater benefit than those would confer, who should make a judicious selection from our best authors upon ethics, politics and history, and promote cheap editions of them in Numbers, without waiting until the demand was such as to make the sale a matter of perfect certainty. Lord John Russell, in his excellent and instructive speech upon Parliamentary Reform, delivered in 1822, stated, that ' an establishment was commenced ' a few years ago, by a number of individuals, with a capital of ' not less than a million, for the purpose of printing standard ' works at a cheap rate;' and he added, that it had been ' very ' much checked in its operation by one of those Acts for the sup- ' pression of knowledge which were passed in the year 1819, ' although one of its rules was not to allow the venders of its ' works to sell any book on the political controversies of the ' day.' The only part of this plan which appears at all objectionable, is the restriction upon politics. Why should not political, as well as all other works, be published in a cheap form, and in Numbers? That history, the nature of the constitution, the doctrines of political economy, may safely be disseminated in this shape, no man now-a-days will be hardy enough to deny. Popular tracts, indeed, on the latter subject, ought to be much more extensively circulated for the good of the working classes, as well as of their superiors. The interests of both are deeply concerned in sounder views being taught them; I can hardly imagine, for example, a greater service being rendered to the men, than expounding to them the true principles and mutual relations of population and wages; and both they and their masters will assuredly experience the effects of the prevailing ignorance upon such questions, as soon as any interruption shall happen in the commercial prosperity of the country, if indeed the present course of things, daily tending to lower wages as well as profits, and set the two classes in opposition to each other, shall not of itself bring on a crisis. To allow, or rather to induce the people to take part in those discussions, is therefore not merely safe, but most wholesome for the community, and yet some points connected with them are matter of pretty warm contention in the present times; but these may be freely handled, it seems, with safety; indeed, unless they are so handled, such subjects cannot be discussed at all. Why then may not every topic of politics, party as well as general, be treated of in cheap publications? It is highly useful to the community that the true principles of the constitution, ecclesiastical and civil, should be well understood by every man who lives under it. The great interests of civil and religious liberty are mightily promoted by such wholesome instruction; but the good order of society gains to the full as much by it. The peace of the country, and the stability of the government, could not be more effectually secured than by the universal diffusion of this kind of knowledge. The abuses which through time have crept into the practice of the constitution, the errors committed in its administration, and the improvements which a change of circumstances require even in its principles, may most fitly be expounded in the same manner. And if any man or set of men deny the existence of such abuses, see no error in the conduct of those who administer the government, and regard all innovation upon its principles as pernicious, they may propagate their doctrines through the like channels. Cheap works being furnished, the choice of them may be left to the readers. Assuredly, a country which tolerates every kind, even the most unmeasured, of daily and weekly discussion in the newspapers, can have nothing to dread from the diffusion of political doctrines in a form less desultory, and more likely to make them be both well weighed at the time, and preserved for repeated perusal. It cannot be denied, that the habit of cursory reading, engendered by finding all subjects discussed in publications, which, how great soever their merits may be, no one looks at a second time, is unfavourable to the acquisition of solid and permanent information*.

---

* I am glad to find this task in part most ably executed by my worthy friend Mr. Marshall, of Leeds. He has published a small elementary treatise on the principles of Œconomics for the use of the working classes. It is most ably executed.

Although the publication of cheap works is the most effectual method of bringing knowledge within the reach of a poor man's income, there are other modes deserving our attention, whereby a similar assistance may be rendered, and his resources economized. Circulating libraries may in some circumstances be of use; but, generally speaking, they are little suited to those who have only an hour or two every day, or every other day, to bestow upon reading. *Book Clubs*, or *Reading Societies*, are far more suited to the labouring classes, may be established by very small numbers of contributors, and require an inconsiderable fund. If the associates live near one another, arrangements may be easily made for circulating the books, so that they may be in use every moment that any one can spare from his work. Here, too, the rich have an opportunity presented to them of promoting instruction without constant interference; the gift of a few books, as a beginning, will generally prove a sufficient encouragement to carry on the plan by weekly or monthly contributions; and with the gift a scheme may be communicated, to assist the contributors in arranging the plan of their association. I would here remark the great effect of combination upon such plans, in making the money of individuals go far. Three-halfpence a week laid by in a whole family, will enable it to purchase in a year one of the cheap volumes of which I have spoken above, and a penny a week would be sufficient, were the publications made as cheap as possible. Now, let only a few neighbours join, say ten or twelve, and lend each other the books bought; and it is evident, that for a price so small as to be within the reach of the poorest labourer, all may have full as many books in the course of the year as it is possible for them to read, even supposing that the books bought by every one are not such as all the others desire to have *. The publication of books in Numbers greatly helps this plan; for it enables those who choose to begin it at any time, without waiting until they have laid by enough to purchase a volume in each family; and where books not so published are wanted, booksellers would do well to aid such associations by giving them a year's credit; whatever propagates a taste for reading must secure their interest in the end. In many parts of Scotland, *Parish Libraries* have been formed with a view to the same object. They originated, I believe, in general with the wealthier classes and the farmers; but after laying the foundation

---

* It is found that the average number of volumes read by the members of a Mechanics Institution, in a great town, is between 10 and 11 a year; by the members of a book society, in the villages of an agricultural district, between 5 and 6. Now the cheap books contain between two and three times the matter in the ordinary publications; therefore, it is evident, that such an association as that proposed, would have three times as much reading as is wanted in towns, and five or six times as much as in the country.

by collecting a few books, those persons left the management most wisely to the readers themselves, and required them to pay for the support of the fund and purchase of new books. *Cottage Libraries* upon a somewhat similar plan are beginning to be formed in some parts of England. There is one at Taunton, where the contributors pay only a penny a week, and above a thousand issues of books have been made to 80 persons in the course of a year. The only officers are a treasure and librarian, who attend every Saturday evening, to exchange the books and receive subscriptions. They also select the books; a faulty arrangement in my opinion, unless the officers are themselves chosen by the readers. The obvious and the sound plan is to establish some general regulation respecting the kind of books to be purchased, (which must, in some degree, depend on the circumstances of each association,) and then to let each contributor choose in proportion to what he pays, or to let several join in choosing a book equal in price to their united contributions. If the rich patrons of the scheme wish to interfere with the choice, it should be either by giving books, or choosing in proportion to their pecuniary contribution. But I confess I should be better pleased to see such libraries, after they are once established, left wholly to the support of the readers, who are sure to care for them if they pay for them, long after richer patrons would tire of the details*.

An excellent plan was about ten years ago adopted by Mr. S. Brown, of Haddington, for instructing the towns and villages of the county of East-Lothian, in succession, by means of the same books. It began with only a few volumes; but he now has 19 *Itinerant Libraries* of 50 volumes each, which are sent round the different stations, remaining a certain time at each. For these there are 19 divisions, and 15 stations, 4 divisions being always in use at the chief town, and 2 at another town of some note. An individual at each station acts as librarian. There are 700 or 800 readers, and the expenses, under 60*l.* a year, are defrayed by the produce of a sermon, the sale of some tracts, and subscriptions, in small sums averaging 5*s.* This plan is now adopted in Berwickshire, by Mr. Buchan, of Kelloe, with this very great improvement, that the current expenses are defrayed by the readers, who pay twopence a month, and I hope choose the books. These libraries have given rise to a scientific Institution, as we shall presently see; and it is peculiarly gratifying to observe that the ori-

---

* Since this Pamphlet was first published I am extremely gratified to find that my suggestions have been acted upon at Haverfordwest, where an *Agricultural Book Society* has been formed, under the patronage of Captain Ackland, Mr. Harvey, my friend the Honourable E. Edwardes, M.P., Colonel Scourfield, M.P., and others. The principle which I have ventured to recommend, of allowing each subscriber to name books to the amount of his subscription, has been adopted.

ginal scheme from which the whole has followed, was merely a library for *religious tracts*, established ever since 1810; and into which were afterwards introduced, in perfect consistency with the primary object, some literary and scientific works.

It is, however, not only necessary that the money of the working classes, but their time also, should be economized; and this consideration leads to various suggestions.

In the *first* place, there are many occupations in which a number of persons work in the same room; and unless there be something noisy in the work, one may always read while the others are employed. If there are twenty-four men together, this arrangement would only require each man to work one extra day in four weeks, supposing the reading to go on the whole day, which it would not; but a boy or a girl might be engaged to perform the task, at an expense so trifling as not to be felt. This expedient, too, it may be observed, would save money as well as time; one copy of a book, and that borrowed for the purpose, or obtained from a reading society or circulating library, would suffice for a number of persons. I may add, that great help would be given by the better informed and more apt learners, to such as are slower of apprehension and more ignorant; and discussion (under proper regulations) would be of singular use to all, even the most forward proficients; which leads me to observe,

Secondly, That societies for the express purpose of promoting conversation are a most useful adjunct to any private or other education received by the working classes. Those who do not work together in numbers, or whose occupation is of a noisy kind, may thus, one or two evenings in the week, meet and obtain all the advantages of mutual instruction and discussion. An association of this kind will naturally combine with its plan the advantages of a book club. The members will most probably be such as are engaged in similar pursuits, and whose train of reading and thinking may be nearly the same. The only considerable evils which they will have to avoid, are, being too numerous, and falling too much into debate. From twenty to thirty seems a convenient number; and nearer the former than the latter. The tone ought to be given from the beginning, in ridicule of speech-making, both as to length and wordiness. A subject of discussion may be given out at one meeting for the next; or the chairman may read a portion of some work, allowing each member to stop him at any moment, for the purpose of controverting, supporting, or illustrating by his remarks the passage just read. To societies of this kind master workmen have the power of affording great facilities. They may allow an hour on the days when the meetings are holden; or if that is too much, they may allow the men to begin an hour earlier on those days; or if even that cannot be managed, they may let them have an hour and a half, on condition of working half an hour extra on three other days. But a more essential help will be the giving them a place to meet. There are hardly twenty or thirty workmen in any branch of business, some of whose masters have not a room, workshop, warehouse, or other place sufficient to accommodate such a society: and it is quite necessary that the place of rendezvous should on no account be the alehouse. Whoever lent his premises for this purpose, might satisfy himself that no improper persons should be admitted, by taking the names of the whole club from two or three steady men, who could be answerable for the demeanour of the rest. Any interference beyond this would be unwise: unless in so far as the men might voluntarily consult their masters from time to time; and their disposition to do so must depend wholly upon the relations of kindness and mutual confidence subsisting between the parties. If any difficulty should be found in obtaining the use of a room from their masters, there seems to be no good reason why they should not have the use of any school-room that may be in their neighbourhood; and one room of this kind may accommodate several societies; three, if the meetings are twice a week; and six, if they only meet once. I shall presently illustrate this matter further when I come to speak of the Glasgow Institution.

In the *third* place, it is evident that as want of time prevents the operative classes from pursuing a systematic course of education in all its details, a more summary and compendious method of instruction must be adopted by them. The majority must be content with never going beyond a certain point, and with reaching that point by the most expeditious route. A few, thus initiated in the truths of science, will no doubt push their attainments much further; and for these the works in common use will suffice; but for the multitude it will be most essential that works should be prepared adapted to their circumstances. Thus, in teaching them geometry, it is not necessary to go through the whole steps of that beautiful system, by which the most general and remote truths are connected with the few simple definitions and axioms; enough will be accomplished, if they are made to perceive the nature of geometrical investigation, and learn the leading properties of figure. In like manner, they may be taught the doctrines of mechanics with a much more slender previous knowledge both of geometry and algebra, than the common elementary works on dynamicks pre-suppose in the reader. Hence, a most essential service will be rendered to the cause of knowledge by him who shall devote his time to the composition of elementary treatises on the Mathematics, sufficiently clear, and yet sufficiently compendious, to exemplify the method of reasoning employed in that science, and to impart an accurate knowledge of the most useful fundamental propositions, with their application to practical purposes; and treatises upon Natural Philosophy, which may teach the great principles of physics, and their practical application, to readers who have but a general knowledge of mathematics, or who are even wholly ignorant of the science beyond the common rules of arithmetic. Nor let it be supposed, that the time thus bestowed is given merely to instruct the people in the rudiments of philosophy, though this would of itself be an object sufficiently brilliant to allure the noblest ambition; for what higher achievement did the most sublime philosophy ever aspire after, than to elevate the views and refine the character of the great mass of mankind—at least in later times, when science no longer looks down as of old upon the multitude, supercilious, and deeming that great spirits alone perish not with the body? But if extending the bounds of science itself be the grand aim of all philosophers in all ages, they indirectly, but surely, accomplish this object, who enable thousands to speculate and experiment for one to whom the path of investigation is now open. It is not necessary that all who are taught, or even any large proportion, should go beyond the rudiments; but whoever feels within himself a desire and an aptitude to proceed further, will press forward; and the chances of discovery, both in the arts and in science itself, will be thus indefinitely multiplied. Indeed, those discoveries immediately connected with experiment and observation, are most likely to be made by men, whose lives being spent in the midst of mechanical operations, are at the same time instructed in the general principles upon which these depend, and trained betimes to habits of speculation. He who shall prepare a treatise simply and concisely unfolding the doctrines of Algebra, Geometry, and Mechanics, and adding examples calculated to strike the imagination, of their connexion with other branches of knowledge, and with the arts of common life, may fairly claim a large share in that rich harvest of discovery and invention which must be reaped by the thousands of ingenious and active men, thus enabled to bend their faculties towards objects at once useful and sublime.

Although much may be done by the exertions of individuals, it is manifest that a great deal more may be effected by the labours of a body, in furthering this important measure. The subject has for some time past been under consideration, and I am not without hopes of seeing formed a Society for promoting the composition, publication, and distribution of cheap and useful works. To qualify persons for becoming efficient members of this association, or co-operating with it all over the country, neither splendid talents, nor profound learning, nor great wealth are required. Though such gifts, in their amplest measure, would not be thrown away upon so important a design, they are by no means indispensable to its success. A well-informed man of good sense, filled with the resolution to obtain for the great body of his fellow-creatures, that high improvement which both their understandings and their morals are by nature fitted to receive, may labour in this good work, either in the central institution or in some remote district, with the certainty of success, if he have only that blessing of leisure for the sake of which riches are chiefly to be coveted. Such a one, however averse by taste or habit to the turmoil of public affairs, or the more ordinary strifes of the world, may in all quiet and innocence enjoy the noblest gratification of which the most aspiring nature is susceptible; he may influence by his single exertions the character and the fortunes of a whole generation, and thus wield a power to be envied even by vulgar ambition for the extent of its dominion—to be cherished by virtue itself for the unalloyed blessings it bestows.

Fourthly, The preparation of elementary works is not the only, nor, at first, is it the most valuable service that can be rendered towards economizing the time of the labouring classes. The institution of Lectures is, of all the helps that can be given, the most valuable, where circumstances permit; that is, in towns of a certain size. Much may thus be taught, even without any other instruction; but, combined with reading, and subservient to it, the effects of public lectures are great indeed, especially in the present deficiency of proper elementary works. The students are enabled to read with advantage; things are explained to them which no books sufficiently illustrate; access is afforded to teachers, who can remove the difficulties which occur perpetually in the reading of uneducated persons; a word may often suffice to get rid of some obstacle which would have impeded the unassisted student's progress for days; and then, whatever requires the performance of experiments to become intelligible, can only be learnt by the bulk of mankind at a lecture, inasmuch as the wealthy alone can have such lessons in private, and none but men highly gifted can hope to master those branches of science without seeing the experimental illustrations.

The branches of knowledge to which these observations chiefly apply, are Mechanical Philosophy and Chemistry, both as being more intimately connected with the arts, and as requiring more explanation and illustration by experiment. But the Mathematics, Astronomy, and Geology, the two former especially, are well fitted for being taught publicly, and are of great practical use. Nor is there any reason why Moral and Political Philosophy should not be explained in public lectures, though they may be learnt by reading far more easily than the physical sciences.

In all plans of this description, it is absolutely necessary that the expenses should mainly be defrayed by those for whose benefit they are contrived. It is the province of the rich to lay the foundation, by making certain advances which are required in the first instance, and enabling the poor to come forward, both as learners and contributors. But no such scheme can either take a deep root, or spread over the country so as to produce its full measure of good, unless its support is derived from those who are chiefly to reap the benefits. Those benefits are well worth paying for; they are not only of great value in the improvement and gratification which they afford to the mind, but in the direct addition which they make to the pecuniary resources of the labouring classes. Instruction in the principles upon which the arts depend, will repay in actual profit to those who live by the arts, far more than the cost of learning, An artisan, a dyer, an engine-maker, will gain the more in money or money's worth for being an expert chemist or mechanician; and a farm-servant, or bailiff, for knowing the economy and diseases of cattle. I have before me the extract of a letter from one of the greatest engine-makers in the country, stating, that a young man in humble life had been selected from among many applicants, to fill a considerable place in the manufactory, on account of his proficiency in science. The profit directly accruing from the knowledge of those sciences provides an immediate fund, out of which the cost of acquiring it may be easily defrayed; but a fund is as certainly though somewhat more remotely secured for repaying, with large interest, the expense of acquiring knowledge of a more general description—those branches of learning which improve the morals, expand the understanding, and refine the taste. That invaluable fund is composed of the savings made by substituting pure and harmless and cheap gratifications, in the stead of luxuries which are both grosser and more costly—hurtful to the health, and wasteful of time.

The yearly cost of a lecture in the larger cities, where enlightened and public-spirited men may be found willing to give instruction for nothing, is indeed considerably less than in smaller places, where a compensation must be made for the lecturer's time and work. But it seems advisable, that, even where gratuitous assistance could be obtained, something like an adequate remuneration should be afforded, both to preserve the principle of independence among the working classes, and to secure the more accurate and regular discharge of the duty. We shall therefore suppose, that the lectures, as well as the current expenses of the room, and where there are experiments, of the apparatus, are to be paid for; and still it appears by no means an undertaking beyond the reach of those classes. The most expensive courses of teaching will be those requiring apparatus; but those are likewise the most directly profitable to the scholars. Contributions may be reckoned upon to begin the plan, including the original purchase of apparatus; and then we may estimate the yearly cost, which alone will fall upon the members of the Association. The hire of a room may be reckoned at 30l.; the salary of a lecturer, 40l.; wear and tear of apparatus,

20*l.*; assistant and servant, 10*l.*; clerk or collector, 10*l.*; fire and lamps, 5*l.*; printing and advertising, 15*l.*; making in all 130*l.* But if two, or three courses are delivered in the same room, the expenses of each will be reduced in proportion. Suppose three: the room may probably be had for 50*l.*, the printing for 20*l.*, and the servants for 30*l.*; so that the expense of each course will be reduced to about 100*l.* Each course may occupy six months of weekly lectures; consequently, if only a hundred artisans are to be found who can spare a shilling a week, one lecture may be carried on for 130*l.*; and if 120 artisans can be found to spare a shilling a week, three courses may be carried on during the year, and each person attend the whole. This calculation, however, supposes a very inconsiderable town. If the families engaged in trade and handicrafts have, one with another, a single person contributing, the number of 100 answers to a population of only 770, supposing the proportion of persons engaged in trade and handicrafts to be the same as in the West Riding of Yorkshire; and 710, taking the proportion of Lancashire. If, indeed, we take the proportions in the manufacturing towns, it will answer in some cases to a population of 5500, and in others of little more than 500. But even taking the proportion from towns in the least manufacturing counties, as Huntingdonshire, the population required to furnish 100 will not exceed 900—which supposes a town of about 200 houses. One of three times the size is but an inconsiderable place; and yet in such a place, upon a very moderate computation, 200 persons might easily be found to spare sixpence a week all the year round; which would be amply sufficient for two lectures. In the larger towns, where 500 or 600 persons might associate, five shillings a quarter would be sufficient to carry on three or four lectures, and leave between 150*l.* and 200*l.* a year for the purchase of books.

In estimating the expenses I have supposed a room to be hired and the rent to be moderate. To make a beginning, the parties must make a shift with any public room or other place that may be vacant; the great point is to begin: the numbers are certain to increase, and the income with the numbers, as the plan becomes known and its manifold attractions operate upon the people. For the same reason I reckon a small sum for apparatus. Great progress may be made in teaching with very cheap and simple experiments. Indeed some of the most important, if not the most showy, are the least costly and complicated. By far the grandest discoveries in natural science were made with hardly any apparatus. A pan of water and two thermometers were the tools that in the skilful hands of Black detected latent heat; a crown's worth of glass, threepenny-worth of salt, a little chalk, and a pair of scales, enabled the same great philosopher to found the system of modern chemistry, by tracing the existence and the combinations of fixed air; with little more machinery the genius of Scheele* created the materials of which the fabric was built, and anticipated some of the discoveries that have illustrated a later age; a prism, a lens, and a sheet of pasteboard enabled Newton to unfold the composition of light, and the origin of colours; Franklin† ascertained the nature of lightning with a kite, a wire, a bit of riband, and a key:—to say nothing of the great chemist of our own day, of whose most useful, perhaps most philosophical discovery, the principle might have been traced with the help of a common wire fire-guard. Even the elements of mechanics may be explained with apparatus almost as cheap and simple.—To take one instance; the fundamental property of the lever (and I may say of the whole science) may be demonstrated by a foot rule, a knife, and a few leaden balls of equal size. The other mechanical powers (which are indeed for the most part resolvable into the lever) may be explained with almost equal ease; and after all, it is those principles that practical men most require to have unfolded, and their application to mechanism illustrated, by figures and instruments. Machinery, even in its complicated form, is more easily understood by them, because they are in practice familiar with its operations and terms, and will follow the description of an engine and its working without a model, or at most with a drawing, far more readily than the learners of natural science in other conditions of life. The simplification of apparatus for teaching physical science is an important object, and one to which learned men may most usefully direct their attention. There cannot be a doubt, that a compendious set of machines may be constructed to illustrate at a very cheap price a whole course of lectures. Certain parts may be prepared capable of being formed into various combinations, so as to present different engines; and where separate models are necessary, their construction may be greatly simplified by omitting parts which are not essential to explain the principle, and show the manner of working. The price, too, will be greatly reduced when a larger number being required of each, they may be prepared by wholesale. A friend of mine is at present occupied in devising the best means of simplifying apparatus for lectures upon the mechanical powers; and cheap chemical laboratories may then receive his consideration. It is likewise in contemplation at a great manufacturing establishment, where every part of the machinery is made upon the spot, to prepare a number of sets of cheap apparatus for teaching, so that any Mechanics Institution may on very moderate terms be furnished at least with what is necessary for carrying on a course of dynamics. The drawings may be multiplied by the polygraphic methods generally in use.

The difficulty of obtaining a fit lecturer is one likely for some

---

* A working chemist.   † A working printer.

time to be much felt, especially in small towns. One method of removing it is by sending an experienced teacher from place to place; and the man qualified for the task, who should fastidiously reject so useful and so honourable an occupation, might be a man of science, but would little deserve to be called a philosopher. No talents and no acquirements are too great to be thus applied; and no use to which parts and learning can be put is more dignified. But another supply of instructors will soon be ready. Each Institution now established must in a short time form teachers. Among a great number of students, some must be found to make such progress as will qualify them for the office. In the Edinburgh School of Arts a joiner has for some time past been teaching mathematics, which he learnt there. At Glasgow, a person of the same trade, who had been taught at the school established by Dr. Birkbeck, has lectured on geography, chemistry, and mechanics. These instances prove that the men will be able to teach; it is equally clear that the wages of a lecturer will make them turn their attention to this business in places where one is wanted.

After all, it may often happen that a lecture cannot be undertaken on however moderate a plan; in that case it will be advisable to begin with a library, to which a lecture may afterwards be added.—This was the course pursued at Kendal, where a " *Mechanics and Apprentices Library*" was begun last spring, and in autumn a course of lectures was delivered upon the Philosophy of Natural History. At Carlisle, and I believe at Hawick, the same method has been adopted.

I have remarked, that in forming these Institutions, it is a fundamental principle to make the expenses be mainly defrayed by the mechanics themselves; it is another principle, in my opinion equally essential, that they should have the principal share in the management. This seems necessary for securing both the success and the independence of the system. Nor is there the least reason to apprehend mismanagement. If benefit societies are, upon the whole, well managed, we may rely upon institutions being still better conducted, where the improvement of the mind being the object, those only will ever take an active part, who are desirous of their own advancement in knowledge, and of the general instruction of the class to which they belong. Indeed there seems no better means of securing the continued attention of the Directors, than placing the direction in the hands of those who are alone interested in the prosperity of the concern. Neither is there any fear that the suggestions of persons in a higher station, and of more ample information, may not be duly attended to. Gratitude for the assistance received, and the advice offered, together with a conviction that the only motive for interfering is the good of the establishment, will give at least their just weight to the recommendations of patrons; and if it were not always so, far better would it be to see such influence fail entirely, than to run the risk of the apathy which might be occasioned among the men, and the abuse of the Institutions themselves, which might frequently be produced by excluding from the control of their affairs those whose interests are the only object in view. The opinions of patrons are always sure to have influence as long as their object plainly is to promote the good of those for whom the Institution was founded; and as soon as they are actuated by any other views, it is very fit that their influence should cease. There is nearly as little reason to apprehend, that the necessity of discussing, at meetings of the members, the affairs of the Institution, will give rise to a spirit of controversy and a habit of making speeches. Those meetings for private business will of course be held very seldom; and a feeling may always be expected to prevail, that the continuance of the establishment depends upon preserving union, notwithstanding any diversity of opinion in matters of detail, and upon keeping the discussion of rules and regulations subordinate to the attendance upon the lectures, the main object of the establishment. The time when information and advice is most wanted, with other assistance from the wealthy and the well informed, is at the beginning of the undertaking; and at that time the influence of those patrons will necessarily be the most powerful. Much depends upon a right course being taken at first; proper rules laid down; fit subjects selected for lecture; good teachers chosen; and upon all these matters the opinions and wishes of those who chiefly contribute to found the several institutions, must receive great attention. What I have now stated, is not merely that which seems likely to happen by reasoning from the circumstances; it has in fact happened in the instances where the trial has been made on the largest scale. We have never found any inconvenience from this plan during the twelve months that our Mechanics Institution in London has been established. In Glasgow, there is a much longer experience in its favour; with this addition, that a contrary plan having at one time been pursued there, the men ceased to interest themselves in the lecture; and the Institution declined. The extraordinary success of the new Institution, which now places it at the head of all such establishments, may chiefly be ascribed to its administration being in the hands of the men themselves*.

I have said that the *independence* of these undertakings, as well as their success, is to be considered. I really should be disposed

* It gives me the greatest pleasure to perceive that these principles have been universally adopted since the circulation of this tract. The rule has been laid down in all the institutions formed, that two-thirds of the committee shall be working-men.

to view any advantage in point of knowledge gained by the body of the people, as somewhat equivocal, or at least as much alloyed with evil, if purchased by the increase of their dependence upon their superiors. They will always be abundantly thankful for the help afforded them in beginning such institutions, and quite ready to receive advice from those who render them assistance. But if the latter keep the management entirely in their own hands, they enforce the appeal to gratitude by something very like control; and they hurt the character of those whom they would serve. For this reason, as well as for promoting more effectually and generally the establishment of these institutions, it is of the last importance that the yearly expense should be reduced to such a sum as can be wholly raised by the students. What they receive in money from their superiors will then be given once for all at the outset; what they receive from time to time in good counsel, and in teaching, either by lectures or publications, shows much real kindness, confers a great benefit, and ensures a grateful return, without bringing into action any of those feelings alike painful and injurious, which arise from the assumption of authority grounded on the mere differences of rank and wealth.

It is now fit that we advert to the progress that has already been made in establishing this system of instruction. Its commencement was the work of Dr. Birkbeck, to whom the people of this island owe a debt of gratitude, the extent of which it would not be easy, perhaps in the present age not possible, to describe; for as, in most cases, the effective demand precedes the supply, it would have been more in the ordinary course of things, that a teacher should spring up at the call of the mechanics for instruction : but long before any symptoms appeared of such an appetite on their part, and with the avowed purpose of implanting the desire in them, or at least of unfolding and directing it, by presenting the means of gratification, that most learned and excellent person formed the design, as enlightened as it was benevolent, of admitting the working classes of his fellow-countrymen to the knowledge of sciences, till then almost deemed the exclusive property of the higher ranks in society, and only acquired accidentally and irregularly in a few rare instances of extraordinary natural talents, by any of the working classes. Dr. Birkbeck, before he settled in London, where he has since reached the highest station in the medical profession, resided for some time in Glasgow as Professor in the Anderson College; and about the year 1800, he announced a Course of Lectures on Natural Philosophy, and its application to the Arts, for the instruction of mechanics. But a few at the first availed themselves of this advantage; by degrees, however, the extraordinary perspicuity of the teacher's method, the judicious selection of his experiments, and the natural attractions of the subject, to men whose lives were spent in directing or witnessing operations, of which the principles were now first unfolded to them, proved successful in diffusing a general taste for the study; and when he left Glasgow two or three years afterwards, about seven hundred eagerly and constantly attended the class.

For some time after Dr. Birkbeck's departure, the lectures of his able and worthy successor Dr. Ure were well frequented; and when the number of the students began to decline, probably from the circumstance of their having no direct share in the management of the Institution, the Professor happily thought of adding to it a library for the use of the mechanics, and entrusting the direction of it entirely to a committee chosen by themselves. This gave new life to the enterprise, and the Gas Light Company having in return for some services rendered them by the Professor, agreed to light the book-room two evenings in the week, a custom arose among the men who came to change their books, of remaining to converse upon the subjects of their reading, and an extraordinary impulse was thus given to their spirit of inquiry. The Library Committee, too, being chosen by the whole body, became in some sort its representative, and claimed to interfere in the management of the Institution. It soon happened that some of their suggestions were not attended to; and a difference, at first to be regretted, led to consequences highly beneficial; for a great number seceded from the lectures and formed an Institution entirely under the management of the mechanics themselves. It has been successful beyond all expectation; a thousand working men attended it last winter, while the numbers of the parent establishment were scarcely diminished. Out of these public associations has arisen one upon a more confined but most useful plan, applicable to every large manufactory. The Gas Light Company's men, between 60 and 70 in number, have formed themselves, on the suggestion of Mr. Nelson the foreman, into a club for mutual instruction; laying by a small sum monthly, they have collected about 300 volumes, and the Company giving them a library room, which they light and heat, the men meet every evening, to converse upon literary and scientific subjects, and once a week to lecture; any one who chooses, giving a fortnight's notice that he will treat on some subject which he has been studying. The books are of all kinds, with the exception of theology, which from the various sects the men belong to is of necessity excluded.*

It is somewhat singular, that although there are many towns in Scotland, and some within a short distance of Glasgow, where hundreds of artisans are collected, yet twenty years elapsed

---

* I owe this interesting information to an admirable letter of Mr. D. Bannatyne to Dr. Birkbeck, in the Mechanics Register. Mr. B. as early as 1817 strongly recommended to the country the extension of Dr. B.'s plan, in a valuable paper which he contributed to Mr. M. Napier's Encyclopædia.

before the example was followed, and men profited by an experiment, which, for so long a period, was constantly before their eyes, and attended with such remarkable success. It was not till the year 1821 that Edinburgh adopted the plan with some variations, a part of which appear to be improvements.

The promoters of the measure began by drawing up a short sketch of the proposed institution, and causing it to be circulated among the principal master mechanics, with a request that they would read it in their workshops, and take down the names of such of the men as were desirous of being taught the principles of those sciences most useful to artisans. In the course of ten days, between 70 and 80 names were entered; and a private meeting was held of a few gentlemen who were disposed to encourage the experiment. These resolved to begin a subscription for the purpose. In April 1821 they circulated a prospectus among the mechanics, announcing the commencement of a Course of Lectures on Mechanics, and another on Chemistry, in October following,—with the opening of a Library of Books upon the same subjects, for perusal at home as well as in the room; the hours of lecture to be from eight to nine in the evening, twice a week, for six months; and the terms of admission to the whole, both lectures and library, fifteen shillings a year. A statement was then issued to the public at large, announcing the establishment of a " School of Arts," with the particulars of the plan; and so well was it received, by all classes, that in September, notice was given of 220 mechanics having entered as students, and such a sum having been subscribed by the public, as enabled the Directors to open the establishment in October. When 400 had purchased tickets, the two courses of lectures were delivered by Dr. Forbes and Mr. Galbraith; to which one on architecture and one on farriery were added, with a class for architectural and mechanical drawing during the summer recess.

The Mechanical Lectures had hardly begun, when some of the students, finding the want of mathematical knowledge, proposed to form themselves into a class, under one of their own number, a joiner, who had agreed to teach them gratuitously the Elements of Geometry and the higher branches of Arithmetic. This suggestion was warmly approved of by the Directors, and some assistance in books being given, thirty met once a week for Geometry, and once for Arithmetic; and adopting the plan of mutual instruction, they arranged the class in five divisions, each under the best scholar as a Monitor, and going over in one night the lessons of the night before. The number of this class being limited to thirty, those who were excluded formed another on the same plan, under a cabinet-maker, also a student of the School of Arts. The joiner's name is James Yule; the cabinet-maker's, David Dewar; and their successful exertions to teach their fellow-workmen are deserving of very great commendation. Mr. Galbraith, the Mechanical Professor, adopted the plan of setting exercises to his pupils; and a list has been published of those who chiefly distinguished themselves by the number and accuracy of their solutions, being 25 persons.

The average receipts of the two first years were, from subscriptions, 448*l.* yearly, and from the students 300*l.* The average expenditure was about 620*l.*, and a saving of 300*l.* was made towards building a lecture-room. The expenditure includes, for furniture and apparatus, 216*l.* a year; for books and binding, 110*l.*; and for expenses incident to the subscriptions, as advertisements, collection and meetings, about 70*l.*;—leaving, of current necessary expenses, about 220*l.* only: so that, if the extrinsic subscriptions were at an end, or were confined to the accumulation of a fund for building, the students could themselves carry on the establishment, and have a surplus of 80*l.* a year for the wear and tear, and increase, of the apparatus and the library; and if their contributions were increased to a pound yearly, which would probably make very little, if any, difference in the numbers of students, an additional 100*l.* would be afforded for the better payment of the Lecturers, or, if they continue satisfied, for the establishment of new lectures. This statement is important, as confirming the calculation formerly given, and showing, that, in places where the rich are less liberally inclined than in Edinburgh, the same invaluable establishments may easily be formed and perpetuated, by a judicious encouragement given at first to the mechanics, and without the necessity of relying upon continued assistance from those who first promoted and aided them.*

As nothing can be more useful to the community of that great and enlightened city than the formation of this establishment, so nothing can be more honourable to the inhabitants than the zeal and the harmony with which all ranks have united in conducting it, and all parties among the rich in giving it their support. To Mr. Leonard Horner, in particular, with whom the plan originated and who has principally had the superintendence of its execution, the most grateful acknowledgments are deservedly due; and I trust I may so far use the privilege of ancient friendship, as to express my conviction that there is no one exertion in which his greatly lamented brother would, had he been preserved to us, have borne a deeper interest, and no object which he would more willingly have seen connected with his name.

---

* It has been thought proper to vest the management of this institution wholly in the subscribers. Local considerations, of which I cannot pretend to be a judge, may have rendered this necessary, but it seems, according to the most obvious principles, inconsistent with the prosperity and permanence of the plan.

The complete success of Dr. Birkbeck's plan both at Glasgow originally, and afterwards in a place abounding far less with artisans, very naturally suggested the idea of giving its principles a more general diffusion by the only means which seem in this country calculated for universally recommending any scheme—its adoption in London. An Address was published by Messrs. Robertson and Hodgkin, in the Mechanics Magazine, October 1823; and the call was answered promptly by Dr. Birkbeck himself, and other friends of education, as well as by the master mechanics and workmen of the metropolis. A meeting was held in November; the Mechanics Institution was formed; a sub-scription opened; and a set of regulations adopted. Of these by far the most important and one which in common, I believe, with all my colleagues, I consider to be altogether essential, pro-vides that the committee of management shall be chosen by the whole students, and consist of at least two-thirds working men. The plan was so speedily carried into execution, that in January Dr. Birkbeck, our president, most appropriately opened the Institution with an introductory address to many hundred work-men, crowding from great distances in the worst season and after the toils of the day were over, to slake that thirst of know-ledge which forms the most glorious characteristic of the age; nor was the voluntary offer of a course of lectures upon Me-chanics less appropriate on the part of Professor Millington, who with an honest pride declared to his audience, that he had originally belonged to the same class with themselves. In the course of the year, lectures were delivered by Mr. Phillips on Chemistry, Mr. Dotchin on Geometry, Dr. Birkbeck on Hydrostatics, Mr. Cooper on the application of Chemistry to the Arts, Mr. Newton on Astronomy, Mr. Tatum on Electricity, and Mr. Black on the French language, to great and increasing numbers of workmen. About a thousand now belong to the Institution, and pay 20s. a year. Temporary accommodation has hitherto been provided at the chapel in Monkwell-street, formerly Dr. Lindsey's; and if upon such a subject we might make any account of omens, surely a scheme for the improvement of mankind could not be com-menced under happier auspices than in the place which so vir-tuous and enlightened a friend of his country had once filled with the spirit of genuine philanthropy and universal toleration. But extensive premises have been procured in Southampton Build-ings, for the permanent seat of the Institution; and the founda-tion has been laid there of a spacious lecture-room, and other suitable apartments for the library and apparatus. The sum re-quired for these buildings exceeds three thousand pounds; and it has been generously advanced by Dr. Birkbeck. Others have made presents of money, books, and apparatus; and I should mention with greater admiration the gift of a thousand pounds from Sir Francis Burdett, but that those who know him and who mark his conduct, have so long since become accustomed to such acts of wise and splendid benevolence, that they cease to make us wonder. Let me further express my conviction, founded upon information, that the mechanics of this great city are resolved, as they are well able, to perpetuate and extend the system; nor have I a doubt that they will, even if unassisted, erect other Institutions in those parts of the town which are too remote to benefit by the parent establishment.

The proceedings in London gave a great and general impulse to the friends of education in the country, and the town of New-castle-upon-Tyne was the first to profit by it. An Institution for the instruction of mechanics by books, lectures, and scientific meetings, was established in March 1824, and the first meeting was held, under the auspices of Mr. Turner, who opened it with an excellent address on the 11th of May. The members are admitted by ballot; but any person paying 12s. a year is eligible; and the Committee of Management consists of the workmen as well as their masters. The library consists already of 600 or 700 volumes. Beside benefactors, there are 240 subscribing members, and the meetings for discussion are held monthly; at these, papers are read and conversations entertained upon any scientific or literary subject, with two exceptions only—*controversial* divinity and *party* politics. A fund is forming for the purchase of appara-tus, and lectures will soon be commenced. Mr. Turner, in-deed, several years before the establishment of the society, had lectured upon Natural Philosophy to the working classes. The Literary Society which has long flourished at Newcastle, sup-ported by the rich, must have contributed greatly to the love of knowledge which is now diffusing its blessings among the other classes; and the excellent principle which it adopted of vesting no property or privileges in those who paid a sum by way of admission money, but extending an equal share in its manage-ment and advantages to yearly subscribers, has been strictly acted upon by the founders of the new institution.

It is remarkable that the next example in point of time should be furnished by so inconsiderable a town as Kendal, of not more than 8000 inhabitants; and this instance is the more instructive because it shows how the system may be carried into effect with most limited resources. In April 1824, it was resolved to form a " *Mechanics and Apprentices Library and Institute;*" of which any person paying to the amount of three guineas in money or books, or 4s. yearly, might become a member and be eligible as well as vote for the Committee of Management. There are 150 subscribing members, all of the working classes, beside 50 or 60 by payment for life. The library already amounts to 300 or 400 volumes; and I have a letter before me from the worthy president, Mr. S. Marshall, stating that "the books are nearly all out at a time, such is the ardour for information." Original papers upon subjects of science and literature are read at the Quarterly Meetings; no topics being excluded from discussion except those of a polemical and party nature. A course of lectures was delivered upon the Philosophy of Natural History last autumn, and one on Mechanics will be given this spring; probably one on Chemistry also. " Great delight is stated to have been expressed by the students who attended the lectures." Except that perhaps the meetings are too few, and the yearly subscription lower than might easily be afforded, the plan of this Institution is one of the best I have yet seen; and those errors, the last especially, are on the safe side, and may easily be corrected as the want of funds for lectures and apparatus may require, and the pleasure and profit attending a scientific education shall be more and more felt.

The principles upon which this flourishing Institution was founded have since been acted upon at Carlisle; and the fundamental one, which on every account is the most steadily to be kept in view, has been wisely recognized by a formal resolution, " that such institutions are likely to be most stable and useful " when chiefly conducted by the mechanics themselves;" and by a rule that two-thirds of the committee, consisting of 21, shall be operative mechanics; the payment of five guineas, and a guinea a year for seven years makes a life member; the others pay 8s. a year, and are admitted by the committee by ballot, and their sons or apprentices have all the benefits of the Institution. Above 300 volumes have been collected since November; 155 members have joined the Institution; a course of lectures on Natural Science has been delivered by Mr. Nichol; and the workmen, who had attended it with increasing delight, presented him at the close with a silver box, of four guineas value, with twelve pounds inclosed. The secretary, Mr. Dunbar, has been applied to by some good men in Dumfries, for information upon the manner of establishing a similar institution in that town; and I have a confident expectation that the example will be followed by Whitehaven, if not by the smaller towns. In truth, no place is too small for a mechanics library; and wherever the size will permit, such a beginning is sure to end in a lecture, or at least in some course of private instruction useful to the workmen. The town of Hawick has not above 4000 inhabitants; yet a mechanics society and library has been established there for some time; and Mr. Wilson, from Edinburgh, went thither in the autumn, and delivered a course of lectures on Natural Philosophy to 200 artisans. Out of the Haddington itinerant libraries there grew a School of Arts in 1821, established by some tradesmen who several years before had formed a society for scientific discussion:

and lectures on mechanics, chemistry and the mathematics, have since been successfully delivered to the workmen by Dr. Lorimer, and Messrs Gunn and Cunningham. In like manner, the example of Newcastle has been followed at Alnwick, a town of only 5000 inhabitants, where a library and a society have been founded by the exertion chiefly of Mr. Johnstone; and I have good reason to believe that the same design is in progress both at Morpeth and Hexham.

The great and wealthy and industrious town of Manchester might well be expected to be among the earliest and most zealous in establishing an Institution. This was resolved upon in April, and ample preparations appear to have been made for carrying the plan into execution—798l. had been received before the end of July; of that sum 243l. were annual donations; and 191 mechanics had entered their names as subscribers, at one pound a year. A library is forming, and preparations making, I believe, for delivering a course of lectures. The management of the Institution, however, is entrusted to Directors chosen by and among the honorary members only, and these are persons who either pay ten guineas at entrance, or a guinea a year, beside the subscription of 20s. It becomes me to speak with great diffidence upon the soundness of views which may have been suggested by local considerations unknown to distant observers; but I cannot avoid expressing my earnest wish that this part of the plan may be reconsidered by the excellent and enlightened men who have promoted so good a work. Perhaps the fact of nearly as many mechanics coming forward to join the societies formed in places like Carlisle and Kendal, upon the opposite principle, as at Manchester, where the population is at least tenfold, and the pursuits far more congenial, and where I know that 1200 of the Mechanics Magazine were sold the first day it appeared, may give some weight to my anxious but most respectful suggestion.

The Mechanics Institution of Leeds has been lately formed, principally through the exertions of Messrs. Gott and Marshall. Any person recommended by two members is admitted upon paying two pounds, and 10s. yearly; and any person for 5s. half-yearly is entitled to all its privileges, except that of taking part in the management. Two pounds seems too high for the admission of the workmen as generally as is desirable: a considerable number of them are no doubt members; and as such both vote and are eligible as directors, but the great majority of voters belong to the higher class. A slight change would remove this difficulty. There are 146 members and 136 subscribers already; books of the value of 500l. are purchased; and every thing is prepared for beginning a lecture, offers of gratuitous assistance having been received. The Institution is a very promising one, and the

number of ingenious and public-spirited men in that neighbourhood ensures its success, provided no impediment be thrown in
the way of a cordial co-operation on the part of the men. The
most exemplary spirit of union among men of very different
parties in religion and politics has been exhibited; and the libe-
rality of the masters is sure to be duly appreciated by those in
their service.

The Institutions which I have hitherto mentioned are formed
avowedly for lectures as well as reading, and most of them have
already been able to establish lectures. Some are by their plan
confined to reading, and have not hitherto contemplated any
further instruction; but they may easily make the step. That
of Liverpool deserves the first notice, as being earliest in point
of time.

The Mechanics and Apprentices Library at Liverpool, established in July 1823, chiefly through the exertions of Mr. E.
Smith, comes ultimately, if I mistake not, from a very illustrious
stock; for it was formed upon the model of the plans which owe
their origin to the Library Company of Philadelphia, founded by
Franklin in 1731, and incorporated in 1742*. In six months 800
volumes were collected, and 400 readers subscribed; the library is
now considerably increased, and there are above 600 readers. The
sum paid is two guineas in money or books, for life, or 10s. 6d. a
year; and every person paying either way has the privilege of
recommending readers, who receive books on the guarantee of
any member. The committee of direction is chosen by the
whole members, and all are eligible. The method of keeping the
different books of receipt, loan, register, guarantee, and cata-
logue, is admirably contrived for the quick and accurate dispatch
of business; and is found so successful in practice, that 700 or
800 books are easily exchanged weekly in a very short time;
250 or 300 volumes being received from and as many given out
to 200 readers in little more than an hour without any confusion.
Where there is so much to commend, I am unwilling to hint at
any imperfection; but certainly a course of lectures might without difficulty be added to this prosperous establishment; and although any mechanic may for half a guinea enjoy all the privileges of a member as the society is now constituted, it is plain

---

* Although the remote origin of these institutions may be traced to Franklin, Mr. W. Wood has the high merit of establishing them on their present
plan and adapting them peculiarly to the instruction of mechanics and apprentices. He founded the first at Boston in 1820; he has had the satisfaction
of seeing the plan adopted in New York, Philadelphia, Albany, and other towns;
and I have now before me a letter in which he says that he has succeeded in
forming one at New Orleans, where he was called on business. His plan is to
obtain loans or gifts of books which almost every one has beyond his own
wants; and he reckons 30,000 volumes thus obtained in different towns, and
as many readers.

that the bulk of the members do not belong to this class, although on the guarantee and recommendation of members, by permission of the committee they partake of its benefits. If all were admitted to the library and management on somewhat lower terms, or to the library and lectures upon those terms a little raised, and none allowed to partake of either for nothing, there can be no doubt that a greater interest would be excited among them, and the Institution be more firmly established and more certain of extending its numbers.

A Mechanics and Apprentices Library was instituted at Sheffield in December 1823, and opened in the February following, under the able and zealous superintendence of Mr. Montgomery, a name well known in the literary world, and held in deserved honour by philanthropists. The rules appear to me most excellent. In the workmen is vested the property, in shares of 5s. each paid at first, and they afterwards pay 6s. a year; they form the class of *proprietors;* the others, the *honorary* members, present gifts in money and books, and may, if chosen by the body at large, fill the offices, but have no share in the property. The committee may consist entirely of proprietors; and must have two-thirds from that body. Apprentices have the use of the books for 4s. yearly. The librarian is to attend daily and have the care of the property; he is therefore paid: perhaps this might be rendered unnecessary by adopting some of the judicious regulations established at Liverpool, and exchanging the books once a week. Every donor of a book must write his name in it, as a kind of check; and a rule has been made, as I understand, after a very thorough and somewhat earnest discussion, giving an appeal against the admission of books to the ministers of the different denominations who are subscribers; this rule has however never yet been acted upon. Members lose the benefits of the society if in the workhouse or in prison; but are restored when liberated without payment of their arrears. Of this admirable institution there are now 360 members; of whom 310 are proprietors, and the numbers of these increase daily. There are 1400 volumes, including some most liberal donations; all collected in nine months; and 30 apprentices receive the benefits of the society on the terms already stated. A library and philosophical society has long flourished at Sheffield, and now reckons 350 members, almost all manufacturers and tradesmen. Lectures are occasionally given in it, and I rejoice to hear that there is an arrangement in agitation for admitting the workmen to the benefit of these as soon as the new premises are ready. A letter now before me relates an interesting anecdote for the encouragement of this design. " We have " in our employment a common cutler who found leisure in a " bad time of trade to amuse himself with entomology, and who

" has made great progress in arranging a collection of insects
" for our museum. Another youth in an obscure station is pre-
" paring specimens of our Flora for the same. Ingenious me-
" chanical models have been repeatedly brought before us by
" persons from whom little beyond ordinary handicraft could
" have been expected." The first two circumstances here mentioned strongly confirm the opinion which I have expressed
elsewhere*, and which was grounded on actual observation of Mr.
Fellenberg's establishment in Switzerland, that a high degree of
intellectual refinement and a taste for the pleasures of speculation, without any view to a particular employment, may be
united with a life of hard labour, even in its most humble
branches, and may both prove its solace and its guide.

There are other Mechanics Institutions respecting which I
have not the details, as the very thriving one at Aberdeen, which
has a library of 500 volumes, a valuable apparatus, and a lecture-room for 600 students, where extensive courses on chemical and mechanical science have been delivered. At Norwich a
meeting was lately held, and attended by the most respectable
inhabitants of all sects and parties, in order to found a Mechanics
Institution. The zeal and information displayed there, leave no
doubt whatever of the plan succeeding. Dr. Yelloly stated that
the rules of the London Institution had been communicated by
Dr. Birkbeck. The correspondence of our London Institution
with different parts of the country shows that similar plans are
in contemplation in various other districts of England. It should
seem that a little exertion alone is wanting to introduce the system universally; and this is the moment beyond all doubt, best
fitted for the attempt, when wages are good, and the aspect of
things peaceful. But if in any part of the kingdom more than
another the education of the working classes is of importance,
that part surely is Ireland. I have learned, then, with inex-
pressible satisfaction, that there the system has already been introduced. In Dublin a Mechanics Institution has been established with the soundest views, the great and cardinal principle being
recognised of taking two-thirds of the Directors from the body of
the workmen. A similar plan has been adopted at Cork; and I
have reason to hope that Limerick and Belfast will follow so excellent an example.

To encourage good men in these exertions—to rouse the indiffe-
rent and cheer the desponding by setting plain facts before them—
has been the object of these details. The subject is of such inestimable importance that no apology is required for anxiously addressing
in favour of it all men of enlightened views, who value the real
improvement of their fellow-creatures, and the best interests of

---

* Evidence before the Education Committee, 1818.

their country. We are bound upon this weighty matter to be instant, in season and out of season. I now speak not merely of seminaries for teaching mechanics the principles of natural and mathematical sciences, but of schools where the working classes generally may learn those branches of knowledge which they cannot master by private reading. It must be a small town indeed, where some useful lecture may not, with a little exertion and a little encouragement, be so established that the quarterly contributions of the students may afterwards suffice to continue it. Moral and political philosophy may be acceptable even where there is no field for teachers of chemistry and mechanics; and where no lecture at all can be supported, a library may be set on foot, and the habit of useful reading encouraged. We constantly hear of public-spirited individuals; of men who are friendly to the poor and the working classes; of liberal-minded persons, anxious for the diffusion of knowledge and the cultivation of intellectual pursuits. But no one has a right to assume such titles—to take credit for both zeal and knowledge—if he has done nothing in his own neighbourhood to found a popular lecture, or, should the circle be too narrow for that, to establish a reading club, which, in many cases, will end in a lecture. For such a club, there is hardly a village in the country too small; and I have shown that towns of a very moderate size may support a lecture. After the success of the experiments already made, indeed, it seems little less than shameful that there should be any considerable town without establishments for popular education. I speak from the actual history of some of the instances which I have cited, when I say that one man only is wanted in each place to ensure the success of the plan. Where there is such a man, and workmen in sufficient numbers,—there are all the materials that can be required. He has but to converse with a few master-workmen; to circulate, in concert with them, a notice for a meeting; or if it be deemed better to have no meeting, let them ascertain how many will attend a class; and the room may be hired and the lecturer engaged in a month. The first cost will be easily defrayed by a subscription among the rich; or, if that fail, the collection of a library will be made by degrees out of the money raised by the students. The expense of providing apparatus ought not to deter any one from making the attempt. I have shown how much may be done with but little machinery, and a skilful lecturer can give most useful help to private study, by drawings and explanations, with hardly any experiments at all. The facilities too will increase; the wish for scientific education will beget an effectual demand, and teachers will present themselves to supply the want. Already it would be a safe adventure for a lecturer to engage in, where there are great bodies of artisans. In any of the large manufacturing towns of Lancashire and

Yorkshire, a person duly qualified to teach the principles of mechanics and chemistry, and their application to the arts, would now find it easy to collect a large class, willing and able to remunerate him for his trouble; and it is highly probable, that, before long, there will be established, in each of those places, permanent teachers upon private speculation.

But, great as the disposition to learn already is among the working classes, and certain as a lecture would be of attendants wherever it was once set on foot, there is still a necessity for the upper classes coming forward to assist in making the first step. Those seminaries are still too new; they are too little known among the artisans generally to be thought of and demanded by themselves; still more difficult would it be for them to set about forming the plans for themselves. Even in the largest towns, it is hardly to be expected that the workmen should yet concert measures for their own instruction, although sufficiently numerous to require no pecuniary assistance in procuring the necessary teachers. The present then is the moment for making an effort to propagate the system; and for giving that encouragement which may at once spread those Institutions and render universally habitual the desire of knowledge that already prevails. Nor can the means be wanting among the upper, or even the middle ranks of society. There exist ample funds at present applied to charitable purposes, which at best are wasted, and more frequently employed in doing harm. I speak not now of the large revenue, a million and a half or more from endowments, which is almost altogether expended in a manner injurious to the community; not above a third part belonging to charities connected with education, and of that third by far the greatest portion going to maintain poor children, which is nearly the worst employment of such funds; while of the remaining two thirds, only a very small proportion is spent on perhaps the only harmless objects of common charity, hospitals for the sick poor, or provision for persons ruined by grievous and sudden calamities. But I allude to the large sums yearly collected in every part of the country to support charitable institutions; and, though given from the best of motives, yet applied to increase the number of the poor almost as certainly as the parish rates themselves. These funds are entirely under the control of the contributors; and to them I would fain address most respectfully a few words.

Every person who has been accustomed to subscribe for the support of what are commonly called charities, should ask himself this question. ' However humane the motive, am I ' doing any real good by so expending my money? or am I not ' doing more harm than good?' In either case, indeed, harm is done; because, even if the money so applied should do no mischief, yet, if it did no good, harm would be done by the waste.

But in order to enable him to answer the question, he must reflect, that no proposition is more undeniably true than this, that the existence of a known and regular provision for the poor, whether in the ordinary form of pensions, doles, gratuities, clothing, firing, &c., or in the shape of maintenance for poor children, in whole, or only in part, as clothing, has the inevitable tendency to bring forward not only as many objects as the provision will maintain, but a far greater number. The immediate consequence of such provisions is, to promote idleness and poverty beyond what the funds can relieve: the continued and known existence of the provisions trains up a race of paupers; and a provision for children, especially, promotes improvident marriages, and increases the population by the addition of paupers. It is therefore a sacred duty which every one owes to the community, to refrain from giving contributions to begin such funds; and if he has already become a yearly contributor, it is equally his duty to withdraw his assistance, unless one condition is complied with,—namely, that no new objects shall be taken into the establishment, but that those only who at present belong to it shall be maintained; so that the mischief may be terminated within a limited time, and nothing unfair or harsh done towards those who had previously depended on its funds. I remember the time when money given to beggars was supposed to be well bestowed—a notion now exploded; yet even this exercise of benevolence is less mischievous than the support of regular establishments for the increase of paupers*.

The wise and considerate manner of proceeding which I venture to recommend, would speedily place at the disposal of charitable and enlightened individuals ample funds for supporting works of real, because of most useful charity. Let any one cast his eye over the Reports of the Education Committee and Charity Commissioners, and he may form some idea of the large funds now profusely squandered under the influence of mistaken benevolence. Of the many examples that might be given, let one suffice; its history is in the Report of 1816. The income was above 2000*l.*, of which 1500*l.* arose from yearly subscriptions and donations. This large fund clothed 101 boys, and maintained 65 girls; but the expense of boarding and clothing the girls was of course by far the greatest part of it, perhaps 1200*l.* Much abuse appeared to have crept into the management, in consequence of tradesmen acting as trustees, and voting on the orders to themselves, and on the payment of their own accounts. It was deemed right to check this; and a rule was adopted, at a meeting of trustees, to prevent so scandalous a practice for the future. It was, however, rejected at a meeting of the sub-

---

* Letter to Sir S. Romilly, 1818.

ribers, for which, in all probability, the tradesmen had made a canvass, and obtained the attendance of friends. Nay, a most learned and humane Judge, who was one of the trustees, having afterwards proposed a resolution merely to forbid any trustee or subscriber voting on matters in which he was personally interest-ed, it 'was rejected instantly, and therefore not recorded on the minutes;' whereupon his lordship abstained from attending any future meeting, and, I trust, from ever contributing to the fund. This is one instance only of thousands, where the money collected from well-disposed persons, who take no further charge of a charity than to pay their subscriptions, is wasted by the jobbing of too active and interested managers. But suppose there had been no direct abuse, and that all the income had been honestly and carefully employed in promoting the objects of the establishment, by far the greater part of it would have been hurt-ly bestowed. Instead of clothing 101 boys, and maintaining 65 girls, at the rate of 2000*l.* a year, the fixed income alone of 500*l.* might have educated a thousand children, and left 1500*l.* a year free for establishing other schools, if wanted: and as two others of the same size would in all probability have more than sufficed to supply the defect of education which appears by the report of the West London Lancaster Association to exist in that district, and would have remained sufficient to support an institution for the instruction of 700 or 800 mechanics. Thus, the same money which is now not uselessly, but perniciously bestowed, might, with a little care, and a due portion of steadiness in resisting the interested clamours of persons who subscribe for the purpose of turning it to their own profit, be made the means of at once educating all the children in the worst district of London, and of planting there the light of science among the most useful and industrious class of the community. Now, within the same district, or applicable to it, there are probably other charitable funds, arising from voluntary contribution, to five or six times the amount of this single charity, and it is most likely that there is hardly one of the benevolent individuals who support it but contributes to one or more charities besides. How important, then, does it become for each man carefully to reconsider the use he is making, or suffering others to make, of that money which his humanity has set apart for the relief of his fellow-creatures, and the improvement of their condition; and how serious a duty is it to take care that what originates in the most praiseworthy motives should also end in results really beneficial to the objects of his bounty!

———

I rejoice to think that it is not necessary to close these obser-vations by combating objections to the diffusion of science among

c

the working classes, arising from considerations of a politica
nature. Happily the time is past and gone when bigots could
persuade mankind that the lights of philosophy were to be ex
tinguished as dangerous to religion; and when tyrants could
proscribe the instructors of the people as enemies to their power
It is preposterous to imagine that the enlargement of ou
acquaintance with the laws which regulate the universe, ca
dispose to unbelief. It may be a cure for superstition—fo
intolerance it will be the most certain cure; but a pure an
true religion has nothing to fear from the greatest expansio
which the understanding can receive by the study either o
matter or of mind. The more widely science is diffused, th
better will the Author of all things be known, and the les
will the people be " tossed to and fro by the sleight of men, an
" cunning craftiness, whereby they lie in wait to deceive." T
tyrants, indeed, and bad rulers, the progress of knowledge amon
the mass of mankind is a just object of terror: it is fatal to then
and their designs; they know this by unerring instinct, and un
ceasingly they dread the light. But they will find it more eas
to curse than to extinguish. It is spreading in spite of them
even in those countries where arbitrary power deems itself mo
secure; and in England, any attempt to check its progress woul
only bring about the sudden destruction of him who should b
insane enough to make it.

To the Upper Classes of society, then, I would say, that th
question no longer is whether or not the people shall be i
structed—for that has been determined long ago, and the decisio
is irreversible—but whether they shall be well or ill taught—ha
informed or as thoroughly as their circumstances permit and thei
wants require. Let no one be afraid of the bulk of the commu
nity becoming too accomplished for their superiors. Well edu
cated, and even well versed in the most elevated sciences, the
assuredly may become; and the worst consequence that can fo
low to their superiors will be, that to deserve being called the
betters, they too must devote themselves more to the pursuit
solid and refined learning; the present public seminaries mu
be enlarged; and some of the greater cities of the kingdom, e
pecially the metropolis*, must not be left destitute of the regul
means within themselves of scientific education.

---

* Since this work was first published, I am very happy to say that conside
able progress has been made in maturing a plan for improving the educatio
of the middle and upper classes, by establishing a University in London. Th
this great city should so long have remained with the benefits of scientif
education accessible only to the very small portion of its wealthiest classe
and beyond the reach of above a million of its inhabitants, seems hardly cred
ble. Such a grievance could only have been submitted to through the invet
rate habit which men are apt to get into of conceiving that no one thing ca

To the Working Classes I would say, that this is the time when by a great effort they may secure for ever the inestimable blessing of knowledge. Never was the disposition more universal among the rich to lend the requisite assistance for setting in motion the great engines of instruction; but the people must come forward to profit by the opportunity thus afforded, and they must themselves continue the movement once begun. Those who have already started in the pursuit of science, and tasted its sweets, require no exhortation to persevere; but if these pages should fall into the hands of any one at an hour for the first time stolen from his needful rest after his day's work is done, I ask of him to reward me (who have written them for his benefit at the like hours) by saving threepence during the next fortnight, buying with it Franklin's Life, and reading the first page. I am quite sure he will read the rest ; I am almost quite sure he will resolve to spend his spare time and money, in gaining those kinds of knowledge which from a printer's boy made that great man the first philosopher, and one of the first statesmen of his age. Few are fitted by nature to go as far as he did, and it is not necessary to lead so perfectly abstemious a life, and to be so rigidly saving of every instant of time. But all may go a good way after him, both in temperance, industry and knowledge, and no one can tell before he tries how near he may be able to approach him.

---

be arranged otherwise than they have been used to see it. It cannot be borne much longer ; nor is the establishment of a great public school now problematical upon a like plan, combining cheap education with the inestimable advantage of parental superintendence. The only benefit that I have ever heard ascribed to a premature emancipation of children is, that it is supposed to give them manly habits. I never saw any want of manly feelings at the proper age, that is the years of manhood, among boys educated in the Scotch public schools, where they eat, and sleep, and spend their Saturdays and Sundays at home. Nor have I ever known in those seminaries such scenes of early manhood as have lately disgraced one of our public seminaries, and brought almost equal disgrace upon the administration of criminal justice in England.

THE END.

LONDON:
PRINTED BY RICHARD TAYLOR, SHOE-LANE.

www.ingramcontent.com/pod-product-compliance
Lightning Source LLC
Chambersburg PA
CBHW081307040426

42452CB00014B/2693